A Reader's
Theater Script
and
Guide

一看就会
少儿英语小剧场

农场与王国

主　编　杜效明
副主编　闵　璇
编　委　潘晨曦　凌　凝　杨德俊　周莹莹　张玉霞
　　　　张文慧　慕媛媛　吴　昊　赵　芹　吴秀玲
　　　　冯　会　余晓琴　都兰芳

APTIME 时代出版
时代出版传媒股份有限公司
安徽科学技术出版社

图书在版编目（CIP）数据

农场与王国 / 杜效明主编. --合肥：安徽科学技术出
版社，2022.1
（一看就会演的少儿英语小剧场）
ISBN 978-7-5337-8465-2

Ⅰ.①农⋯　Ⅱ.①杜⋯　Ⅲ.①英语-少儿读物
Ⅳ.①H319.4

中国版本图书馆 CIP 数据核字（2021）第 124071 号

NONGCHANG YU WANGGUO

农　场　与　王　国

主　编　杜效明
副主编　闵　璇

出 版 人：丁凌云　　选题策划：张　雯　周璟瑜　　责任编辑：郑　楠
责任校对：李　茜　　责任印制：廖小青　　　　　　装帧设计：武　迪
出版发行：时代出版传媒股份有限公司　　http://www.press-mart.com
　　　　　安徽科学技术出版社　　　　　　http://www.ahstp.net
（合肥市政务文化新区翡翠路 1118 号出版传媒广场，邮编：230071）
电话：（0551）63533330
印　　制：合肥锦华印务有限公司　　电话：（0551）65539314
（如发现印装质量问题，影响阅读，请与印刷厂商联系调换）

开本：710×1010　1/16　　　印张：5.25　　　字数：105 千
版次：2022 年 1 月第 1 版　　2022 年 1 月第 1 次印刷

ISBN 978-7-5337-8465-2　　　　　　　　　　定价：28.00 元

推荐序

  "一看就会演的少儿英语小剧场"系列图书是一套以英语短剧为表现形式的双语读物，选编了8个家喻户晓的童话故事，故事幽默诙谐，富有戏剧性；语言地道，童趣盎然，并提供发音纯正的音频，带来真实、生动的情境体验。

  本系列图书集自主阅读、分角色朗读、戏剧表演等多种功能于一体，学生可以通过剧本诵读、戏剧表演和贯穿其中的互动合作，获得语言感知、语言理解、语言运用和语言鉴赏的多种体验，在语言、情感、思维、文化意识等多方面获得整体提升。

  英语小剧场是一场由想象力构建的活动，它和普通而枯燥的死记硬背型阅读活动有本质区别。《义务教育英语课程标准》提出，小学生除了简单的听、说、读、写，还应能够进行英语表演。生动有趣的戏剧表演已成为一种以文学作品的口述演绎为中心的综合语言艺术活动。语言在戏剧中是不可或缺的元素，作家通过语言表达戏剧的立意和冲突，演员通过台词表达人物的思想和精神，导演也必须帮助演员处理台词。古希腊时期，许多知名的政治家都要拜演员为师，向演员学习台词功夫，以便提高他们的演说水平。声、台、形、表，基本功对表演艺术来说是缺一不可的，因此演员要具备声乐艺术、语言艺术、舞蹈艺术和表演艺术的修养。作为一种听、说、读、写、思全面发展的活动体验，戏剧表演对学生的英语语言学习和综合素质的提升起到了独特的作用，有助于提高学生的主动阅读能力、批判性思考能力、创意写作能力、精确表达能力、专注倾听能力以及高效的协作能力。

戏剧艺术既是综合艺术（时间和空间艺术的综合），也是集体艺术，需要集体协作才能完成。英国教育学家约翰内森和卡恩认为："运用小组协作的方式来促成学生之间更高级、更深层的互动，这一点尤其重要。"小剧场的表演形式使学生围绕着一个共同的目标进行团队协作，他们可以就内容、角色、舞台表演等细节进行充分讨论沟通。戏剧表演给学生提供了可以广泛参与的学习模式，丰富学生的实践经历，提高学生的团队合作能力。

对于教师而言，也需要一些创新、不同寻常的项目应用于课堂实践。本书中生动有趣的英语短剧，融合了极具时代感的语言表达；随书附赠的《阅读指导》手册，为教师提供具有实操性的说明和指导，帮助策划、实施并完成一场别开生面的戏剧表演活动，开展新颖有趣的第二课堂。学生们可以投入极大的热情且无须耗费太多精力，在相对较短的时间内即可产出一部成熟的舞台作品。本系列图书熔素质教育和英语教学于一炉，是小学英语教学实践的应用范例。

导读

你爱不爱做道具？有没有兴趣来画布景呢？你喜欢表演吗？如果是的话，那么就来排场话剧吧。话剧多有趣啊！话剧是让孩子们学会团队合作的最好的方法！

读者剧场的形式最简单。小读者坐在舞台的椅子上，他们不用背台词，只要把对话有感情地朗读出来便成功啦！

朗读剧场和一般的舞台剧有点儿像。演员们不仅要化装、穿戏服，还要在台上走位，一边说台词一边表演。不过，演员全程是可以看台词的。除此之外，舞台上还要搭布景、放道具。

读者剧场的台本还可以用作木偶剧。小演员站在台幕后，一边移动木偶，一边读对话。

定下话剧形式后，你首先要找到一个足够大的空间来表演。小礼堂的舞台是个不错的选择哟！当然，你也可以在教室里演出。接下来，你要初步定下演出的日期，提交使用舞台的申请。然后，为你的演出做些宣传吧。你可以把宣传单或海报张贴到学校或者社区的布告栏里。

别忘了把这个消息告诉朋友和家人哟！大家都会很期待你的表演的！

show出你的发音
争当英语小明星
▶ 地道口语课
▶ 剧本推荐

微信扫码

目 录

英语小·剧场
展示大舞台

show出你的发音，争当英语小明星

跟我说 · 地道口语课

实用外教口语定制课程，标准英语脱口而出

跟我听 · 剧本推荐

精听好剧本，带你"真听真看真感受"

微信扫码
还可获取本书推荐书单
好书读不停！

门票和剧目单

你可以亲手制作门票和剧目单，也可以用电脑设计它们。不论你选择哪种方法，一定要确定门票上标有剧名、演出日期和具体时间，以及演出地点。

剧目单上应列有节目顺序。剧目单的正面一般印有剧名和演出时间。演员及工作人员的姓名要放在剧目单内页。记得要准备足够的剧目单，并在开演之前把它们发给入场的观众哟。

演员和舞台工作人员

　　一场话剧需要很多人的参与。首先，让我们来分配角色。剧组的每个演员都要配有剧本，并且要熟练地掌握自己的台词。一遍遍地高声朗读你的台词可以让你更快地找到感觉。

　　接下来，需要招工作人员了。一场话剧没有这些重要的工作人员怎么行呢！一个人是可以负责多项工作的。

总导演: 管理人员，布置任务。

服装设计师: 借道具、做服装。

舞台监督: 保障每个环节顺利进行。

灯光设计师: 负责打聚光灯和换光。

布景师: 设计、制作布景。

道具师: 筹备、制作、管理道具。

特效工作人员: 负责音效和特效。

妆容和服装

　　化妆师的工作是整场演出的重中之重！每个参与的演员都是要化妆的，不过，舞台演员化的妆要比我们日常生活中化得浓一点儿。你手边要有基本的彩妆用品，比如睫毛膏、粉底液、腮红和口红等。可以用一次性化妆棉或化妆用棉签给演员上妆，要保证卫生哟！

　　服装设计师需要按照剧情设计服装。他们负责借服装，或者按照每个角色对旧衣服进行改造。借服装或者制作演出服时，你也可以向家长寻求帮助。

3

布景和道具

　　在读者剧场中，道具就是椅子，演员只需要坐在最前面就可以了。相比之下，朗读剧场和一般的舞台剧可就不是这么简单了，布景和道具是必不可少的。

　　布景是为每一幕布置的景物。

　　道具是演员在演出时需要用到的器物。

排演安排和舞台方位

一旦做出上演话剧的决定，就要制作一张彩排时间表喽，并协调大家的时间，尽量在公演之前彩排五次吧。

即便你只需要按照剧本读台词，但是，作为一个团队，你们还是要一起练习。熟练掌握自己的台词后，舞台表演才能更加流畅、自然。没有台词的时候，只要演员还留在台上，就需要做出符合自己角色的动作和表情。

剧本里的舞台方位是从演员的角度得出的，被标注在括号内。表演时，你要面向观众席，所以，左边指的就是你的左手边，右边指的就是你的右手边。

有些舞台术语可能让你摸不着头脑，比如

大幕：舞台的主要幕布，在台口内。

观众席：观众的座位。

侧幕：舞台的左、右边，是藏在观众视线之外的舞台的侧面。

5

故事剧场一

农场安全告急

布景和道具

布景：用硬纸板做的农场和谷仓放在舞台正位，苹果树放在舞台的左侧，舞台上还有农夫琼斯的房子和纸板做的森林。

道具：一大捆干草和几个真苹果或塑料苹果，这些苹果要散落在台上；用硬纸板做成拖拉机，或者也可以把拖车装饰成拖拉机；拖拉机后面还要拉上拖车。

演员表

旁白：讲故事的人。

母鸡亨丽塔：一只迷迷糊糊的鸡。

公鸡"宝刀已老"：外表坚强、内心胆小的公鸡。

小猪"惊恐万分"：总怕挨饿的小猪。

老牛"杞人忧天"：嚼着口香糖、随大流的牛。

小狗"神经过敏"：总想当老大，却跟别的小动物一样胆小。

老狼"诡计多端"：试着把小动物们都骗进它的家。

农夫琼斯：既理智又机警。

妆容和服装

旁白：绒布衬衫配牛仔裤。

母鸡亨丽塔：棕色T恤衫配头饰，头饰上有黄色皮毛做的喙和红色的鸡冠，加上一对用硬纸或皮革做的翅膀。

公鸡"宝刀已老"：红色T恤衫配头饰，头饰上有黄色皮毛做的喙和比母鸡亨丽塔的鸡冠高出几倍的红色鸡冠，加上一对翅膀和用皮革做的尾巴。

小猪"惊恐万分"：粉色T恤衫配用粉色皮革做的猪耳朵，把耳朵粘在发卡上；可以用纸杯当猪鼻子，固定在演员的鼻子上；用粉色毛线绑在铁丝上做出小猪弯弯的尾巴。

老牛"杞人忧天"：黑裤子搭配黑点的白色T恤衫，用毛线编成三股辫，做出一条尾巴来。

小狗"神经过敏"：灰色或黑色的T恤衫；把软软的皮耳朵缝在发卡上，把发卡戴在头上；用皮革做一条尾巴。

老狼"诡计多端"：棕色的 T 恤衫，背后再缝上一条皮尾巴，头上戴一对有皮耳朵的发卡。

农夫琼斯：绒布 T 恤衫，配牛仔裤，头上戴顶草帽。

舞台方位

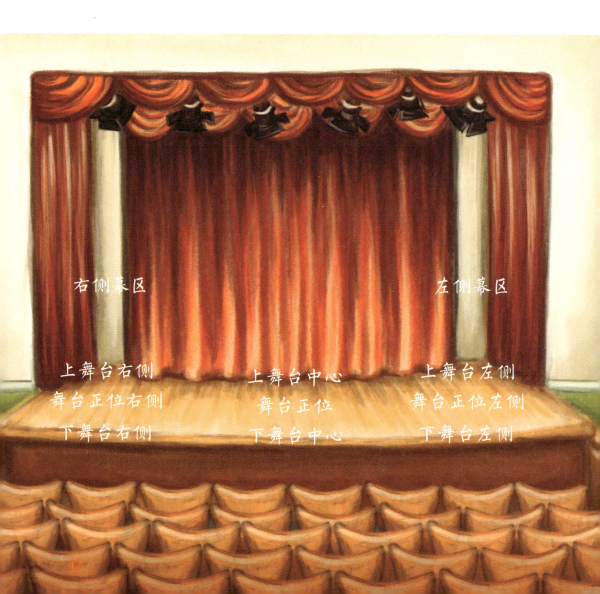

右侧幕区　　　　　　　　　　　　　　　左侧幕区

上舞台右侧　　　　　上舞台中心　　　　上舞台左侧
舞台正位右侧　　　　舞台正位　　　　　舞台正位左侧
下舞台右侧　　　　　下舞台中心　　　　下舞台左侧

Script: Farmyard Security

Scene 1

(Opening of the Curtain: The barn should be at upstage center. An apple tree stands at stage left. The animals are arranged in a large circle. Rusty Rooster is lying on a hay bale. Panicky Pig is asleep by the tractor. Calamity Cow is sleeping by the wagon. The narrator sits on a stool at stage right removed from the action.)

Narrator: Once upon a time, there was a cozy little farm at the edge of a big forest. Most days, the farm was peaceful and quiet. But one day, a very small chicken caused a great big problem. It was late one afternoon and most of the animals were napping. They were dreaming of food buckets full of delicious treats.

(Henrietta Hen enters from stage left and goes over

to sit under the apple tree. She clucks quietly as she walks.)

Narrator: It was warm and sunny. Henrietta Hen decided to nestle under an apple tree in the orchard. She tucked her head under her wing. In just a few minutes, she was sound asleep.

(Henrietta Hen curls up with her head under one arm.)

Narrator: Right above her, the apple tree's branches were loaded with fruit. There were so many apples that all of a sudden, a branch cracked loudly. Several big, red apples fell off the tree. One apple hit Henrietta Hen in the head!

(Loud snapping sound from back stage. Drop three or four apples and let them roll across the stage. Henrietta jumps up and rubs her head.)

Henrietta: *Cluck! Cluck! Cluck!* Oh my goodness, the sky must be falling! I have to tell Farmer Jones right away!

Narrator: Henrietta Hen ran down the path toward the barn, squawking loudly. She found Rusty Rooster sleeping peacefully on a hay bale.

Henrietta: Oh, Rusty Rooster, wake up!

Rusty Rooster: *(Rubbing his eyes)* What is the matter with you? Can't you see I was taking my afternoon nap?

Henrietta: Rusty Rooster, the sky is falling! We have to run and tell Farmer Jones!

Rusty Rooster: *(Looking up)* What do you mean the sky is

falling? Everything looks perfectly all right to me.

Henrietta: It's not all right! I was sound asleep in the orchard and I heard the sky crack. Then a piece of it fell and hit me on the head!

Rusty Rooster: (Looking around nervously and flapping his wings) Oh dear! Well, maybe we should tell Farmer Jones! I'll come along with you.

(Rusty Rooster and Henrietta Hen should lift their knees high as though they are running. They flap their wings and cluck loudly as they walk to Panicky Pig.)

Narrator: The two chickens ran down the road clucking and squawking. They ran to Panicky Pig, who was snoozing by the tractor.

Henrietta: Oh, Panicky Pig, wake up! Wake up! The sky is falling!

Panicky Pig: (Stretches and looks up) What do you mean the sky is falling?

Henrietta: I was sound asleep and I heard it crack. Then a big piece of it fell and hit me on the head!

Panicky Pig: Oh my goodness! That's terrible! What should we do?

Henrietta: We are going to tell Farmer Jones. Do you want to come with us?

Panicky Pig: *(Looking up at the sky and acting frightened)* Of course, I want to come with you! I'm afraid to be caught out here alone when the sky falls down! Do you think we'll be back before dinner?

Henrietta: Don't worry about food! Just hurry!

Narrator: Now the silly chickens and Panicky Pig raced down the road making a lot of noise. Calamity Cow was napping beside the hay wagon.

(Chickens cluck and Pig oinks. They pretend to run as

they approach Calamity Cow.)

Henrietta: Calamity Cow! You have to wake up! The sky is falling! Please come with us to tell Farmer Jones!

Calamity Cow: *(Yawns and looks up)* Don't be ridiculous! How can the sky be falling? It looks perfectly normal to me. It's actually a very pretty blue today with just a few fluffy, white clouds.

Henrietta: I just heard the sky crack! And a big piece of it fell and hit me on the head!

Calamity Cow: *(Looking worried and glancing at the sky)* Oh my, that does sound serious! Maybe I'd better come along, too. There's no sense in taking any chances.

(Henrietta Hen, Rusty Rooster, Panicky Pig, and Calamity Cow exit stage right together.)

剧本：农场安全告急

第一幕

（大幕拉开：谷仓摆在上舞台中心。舞台左侧摆放一棵苹果树。小动物们排成一圈。公鸡"宝刀已老"躺在干草垛上。小猪"惊恐万分"在拖拉机旁睡大觉。老牛"杞人忧天"睡在拖车旁。旁白坐在舞台右侧的椅子上，远离演员。）

旁白：很久以前，森林边有个可爱的小农场，那里的生活既安静又祥和。可是有一天，一只小鸡闯了个通天大祸。故事是这样开始的：傍晚时分，动物们还在睡大觉。它们做着美梦，梦里有数不尽的山珍海味。
（母鸡亨丽塔从舞台左侧上台，走到苹果树下，坐好。母鸡一边走，一边轻轻地发出咕咕声。）
旁白：太阳把农场照得暖洋洋的。母鸡亨丽塔决定在果园的苹果树下休息片刻。她把头缩在了翅膀下。眨眼间，她就睡着了。

(母鸡亨丽塔用一只胳膊护住头。)

旁白：就在她的头上方，一根树枝上结满了沉甸甸的苹果。苹果压弯了枝头，树枝再也承受不住这重量，突然间，发出了"咔"的响声，紧接着，数不清的苹果掉在了地上。一个苹果正好砸在了母鸡亨丽塔的头上！

(后台做出"噼啪"的声效。扔下三四个苹果，让它们在舞台上滚动。母鸡亨丽塔惊跳起来，揉着她的头。)

母鸡亨丽塔：咕咕嗒！咕咕嗒！我的妈呀，天要塌了！我得马上告诉农夫琼斯去！

旁白：母鸡亨丽塔顺着小道直奔谷仓，大声地咕咕惊叫着。她先碰到了正在干草垛上悠闲睡大觉的公鸡——"宝刀已老"。

母鸡亨丽塔：哎呀，"宝刀已老"，快起来吧！

公鸡"宝刀已老"：(揉着眼睛)你慌慌张张地做什么？没看见我正睡午觉呢吗？

母鸡亨丽塔："宝刀已老"，天要塌了！我们得赶紧告诉农夫琼斯去！

公鸡"宝刀已老"：（抬头望天）什么叫"天要塌了"？我觉得一切都挺正常的啊。

母鸡亨丽塔：一点儿都不正常！我本来在果园睡觉，突然间，被天空裂开的声音惊醒了。然后，一块天就砸在了我头上！

公鸡"宝刀已老"：（紧张地向四周张望，扇扇翅膀）我的天哪！你说的对，我们最好赶紧把这个消息告诉农夫琼斯！我跟你一起去。

（公鸡"宝刀已老"和母鸡亨丽塔边高抬腿，边扇动翅膀，高声咯咯、咕咕地叫着跑到小猪"惊恐万分"那儿。）

旁白：两只鸡高声咯咯、咕咕地顺着小道跑到了小猪"惊恐万分"那儿。小猪正在拖拉机旁打着鼾。

母鸡亨丽塔：哎呀，"惊恐万分"，快起来！快起来！天要塌了！

小猪"惊恐万分"：（伸懒腰，抬头看着两只鸡）什么叫"天要塌了？"

母鸡亨丽塔：我本来在睡觉，突然听到了撕裂的声音。然后，一块天直愣愣地砸在了我的头上！

小猪"惊恐万分"：我的天呀！太可怕了！我们该怎么办呢？

母鸡亨丽塔：我们得把这个消息告诉农夫琼斯去。你要不要和我们一起去啊？

小猪"惊恐万分"：（抬头望天，做出惊恐万分的样子）当然要和你们一起去了！我怕天塌下来的时候，把我一个人困在这儿。你觉得咱们晚饭前回得来吗？

母鸡亨丽塔：都什么时候了，还想着吃啊！快点儿走吧！

旁白：于是，两只蠢鸡和小猪"惊恐万分"争先恐后地向农夫琼斯那儿跑去，一路上发出了很大的动静，把睡在拖车旁的老牛——"杞人忧天"惊醒了。

（两只鸡咯咯、咕咕地尖叫，小猪发出哼哼的声音。他们做出急跑的样子，靠近老牛"杞人忧天"。）

母鸡亨丽塔："杞人忧天"！你得起来了！天要塌了！快跟我们去找农夫琼斯吧！

老牛"杞人忧天"：（打了个哈欠后看看天）开什么玩笑啊！天怎么能塌下来呢？我觉得一切都挺正常的啊。今天的天还特别蓝，只有几朵白云。

母鸡亨丽塔：我明明听到了天空裂开的声音啊！之后，一大块天就砸在了我的头上！

老牛"杞人忧天"：（显得有点儿担心，眼睛盯着天空）我的天哪，这可是会要命的呀！我还是跟你们走吧。我可不想冒险。

（母鸡亨丽塔、公鸡"宝刀已老"、小猪"惊恐万分"和老牛"杞人忧天"一起从舞台右侧下台。）

show出你的发音
争当英语小明星
▶ 地道口语课
▶ 剧本推荐

微信扫码

Scene 2

Scene change: Stage crew remove the barn and place farmhouse at upstage center. Henrietta Hen, Rusty Rooster, Panicky Pig, and Calamity Cow all enter stage left.

Narrator: Now all the silly animals raced down the road until they reached Farmer Jones's house. They scrambled up on the porch. Henrietta Hen knocked at the door.

Henrietta: Hello? Hello? Farmer Jones?

(Pause quietly while everyone looks expectantly at the farmhouse.)

Paranoid Puppy: *(Enters stage right)* No one is home, Henrietta.

Henrietta: Oh, *cluck, cluck, cluck*! What will we do now?

Paranoid Puppy: I'm the watchdog. Farmer Jones leaves me in charge of farmyard security while he is away. What's going on?

Henrietta: Oh! There's a terrible problem! We're doomed!

Paranoid Puppy: *(In a brave voice)* Well, you'll be safe here. I'll protect you! We'll wait here on the porch until Farmer Jones comes back.

Panicky Pig: The porch isn't safe! If the sky falls, the

porch will be crushed and so will we!

Paranoid Puppy: Why would the sky fall down? We haven't had a problem with it in years!

Henrietta: Well, I heard it crack and a piece of it hit me on the head. We probably have very little time to save ourselves! Let's head for the woods! There is probably somewhere there that we can hide!

Rusty Rooster: I don't know, Henrietta. Going to the woods doesn't sound safe to me. There are lots of wild animals in the woods.

Henrietta: *(Hands on her hips)* Do you have a better idea?

Rusty Rooster: No, not really.

Henrietta: Well, I'm going to the woods! The rest of you can do whatever you like. *(Henrietta turns and walks off stage right.)*

Panicky Pig: Oh dear, I wish I'd brought a snack! Well, I'm not getting crushed! I'm with her. *(Walks off stage right.)*

Calamity Cow: Me, too! *(Follows Panicky Pig.)*

Rusty Rooster: *(Running after them)* I guess it's better to be safe than sorry.

Paranoid Puppy: *(Looking behind him at the house)* Wait for me! I'm coming, too!

第二幕

　　换布景：舞台工作人员将谷仓移除，把农夫的房子放在上舞台中心。母鸡亨丽塔、公鸡"宝刀已老"、小猪"惊恐万分"和老牛"杞人忧天"一起从舞台左侧上台。

旁白：就这样，所有头脑发昏的小动物们争先恐后地跑向农夫琼斯的房子。它们爬上门廊。母鸡亨丽塔敲起门来。

母鸡亨丽塔：农夫琼斯，你在吗？你在吗？

（大家安静地向农夫家里焦急地张望。）

小狗"神经过敏"：（从舞台右侧上台）家里没人，亨丽塔。

母鸡亨丽塔：糟了，咕咕嗒，咕咕嗒！我们该怎么办啊？

小狗"神经过敏"：我是看门犬。农夫琼斯不在的时候，就由我来负责农场的安全。发生什么事啦？

母鸡亨丽塔：天哪！最糟糕的事情发生了！我们就要

死啦！

小狗"神经过敏"：（勇敢地说）甭担心，在这里你是最安全的，因为，我可以保护你！咱们就待在门廊这儿等农夫琼斯回来。

小猪"惊恐万分"：门廊也不安全呀！要是天塌了，我们和整个门廊都会被压在下面的！

小狗"神经过敏"：天怎么会塌下来呢？我们可从来没有遇到过这么大的天灾啊！

母鸡亨丽塔：是这样的：我先听到了天裂开的声音，紧接着一块天就砸在了我的头上。估计，我们连自救的时间都没有了！让我们去森林里躲一躲吧！或许在那儿，咱们能找到藏身的地方！

公鸡"宝刀已老"：这个……亨丽塔，我不太同意。藏到森林里对我来说一点儿都不安全，那里可有野兽出没呢。

母鸡亨丽塔：（双手叉腰）那你有什么更好的建议吗？

公鸡"宝刀已老"：嗯，这倒真没有。

母鸡亨丽塔：好吧，我要藏到森林里去！你们愿意做什么就做什么吧。（亨丽塔转身从舞台右侧走下台。）

小猪"惊恐万分"：天哪，要是我刚才出门时带份吃的该多好啊！好吧，我可不想被砸死！我要跟亨丽塔去森林里躲起来。(从舞台右侧走下台。)

老牛"杞人忧天"：哎，带上我呀！(紧跟小猪"惊恐万分"。)

公鸡"宝刀已老"：(跟在其他动物身后)我估计，还是藏到森林里保险。

小狗"神经过敏"：(回头看了看房子)等等我！我也去！

show出你的发音
争当英语小明星
▶ 地道口语课
▶ 剧本推荐

微信扫码

Scene 3

Scene change: Stage crew remove the farmhouse and apple tree. Add several cardboard or fake trees to the stage for the woods.

Narrator: Now all those silly animals went down the road to the woods. They were making a lot of noise!

(The animals enter from stage left. The chickens are clucking, the cow is mooing, the pig oinks, and the puppy barks.)

Narrator: Wily Wolf lived on the hill. He heard them coming from a mile away. He slunk down and peered through the trees to see what was going on.

(Wily Wolf appears from stage right and begins to slink around the trees. He pops up in front of the farmyard animals.)

Wily Wolf: Good afternoon, friends!

Animals: OH NO!!! *(Sounding very afraid. All of them back up and fall into a big heap together except*

Henrietta Hen.)

Henrietta: *(Her voice quivering)* Hello, Wily Wolf!

Wily Wolf: Why, Henrietta Hen, what are you doing in my part of the woods?

Henrietta: The sky is falling! We wanted to tell Farmer Jones but we can't find him!

Narrator: Now, wolves are terribly clever. Wily Wolf saw a chance to feed his family for weeks!

Wily Wolf: *(In a sly voice)* Oh, Henrietta, did you say that the sky is falling? Why, that is terrible! Why don't you all come right up to my cave? You'll be safe there if the sky falls.

Rusty Rooster: *(Whispering)* Henrietta, that's a really bad idea!

Henrietta: *(Looking around nervously)* Well, I don't know what to do. We can't stay out here.

Wily Wolf: *(Throws his arms out in welcome)* Henrietta, please don't worry! My cave is the safest place to be if the sky really is falling. And my wife, Fiona, is an extreme couponer! She saves us hundreds of dollars in groceries every month. Our cave is stocked from the floor to the ceiling with food and supplies! You and your friends could live comfortably there with us for years and we would always have enough to eat!

Henrietta: Really?

Panicky Pig: *(Wiping forehead)* Well, that's a relief! We

wouldn't want to run out of food, now would we?

Wily Wolf: My cave is so very warm and cozy. There is

more than enough room for all!

Henrietta: I guess it would be all right, then. *(Pats Wily Wolf on the arm.)* How kind you are. Isn't Wily Wolf kind, Rusty Rooster?

Rusty Rooster: *(Nodding)* He certainly is.

Calamity Cow: Thank you so much, Wily Wolf! We were so lucky that we ran into you today! Can you show us the way to your cave?

Panicky Pig: I'm glad that's decided. I will be so happy to be somewhere safe. Besides, it's almost time for dinner.

Wily Wolf: *(Laughing softly and motioning them forward)* Come right this way, then. Let me welcome you to your new home!

(Animals should make soft noises as they walk in a circular motion around the stage following the wolf.)

Narrator: So Wily Wolf led all the silly animals up the road, through the woods, and to his cave. But just before they were about to go inside, Farmer Jones came walking down the road from the market.

(Farmer Jones enters stage left. Wily Wolf backs away with his hands up.)

Farmer Jones: Stop! Stop! Where are you going, Henrietta Hen?

Henrietta: The sky

is falling! We tried to tell you but we couldn't find you! Wily Wolf offered to take us into his cave where we will be safe. Would you like to come with us?

Farmer Jones: What makes you think the sky is falling?

Henrietta: Well, I heard it crack and a big piece of it hit me on the head!

Farmer Jones: Henrietta, where were you when this piece of sky fell?

Henrietta: I was taking a lovely nap under the apple tree.

Farmer Jones: What did this piece of sky look like?

Henrietta: *(Puts a finger to her forehead as though she is thinking)* Well, let me see if I can remember. It all happened so fast! I think it was big, round, and red!

Farmer Jones: Could it have been an apple that hit you on the head?

Henrietta: Well, let me think. Apples are . . .

Rusty Rooster: *(Speaking slowly and distinctly)* Big and round and red!

Henrietta Hen: Oh! So I guess it could have been . . .

All animals together: An apple!

Panicky Pig: You silly chick! You led us right to the wolf's den!

Wily Wolf: *(Rubbing his hands together)* Yes, she did. So if you will just come inside now, I'll have my wife make dinner! Shall we start with roast chicken tonight?

Farmer Jones: Run!

(Farmer Jones and animals exit stage left, clucking, oinking, mooing, and barking.)

Narrator: And so Henrietta Hen, Rusty Rooster, Panicky Pig, Calamity Cow, Paranoid Puppy, and Farmer Jones ran down the hill to the farm as fast as they could! And poor Wily Wolf, well, he and his wife had to eat veggie burgers for dinner!

The End

第三幕

换布景：舞台工作人员将农夫的房子和苹果树推走。可以用一些硬纸或假树来装扮森林。

旁白：现在头昏脑涨的动物们顺着小径奔向了森林。它们一路上发出了很大的动静！

(小动物们从舞台左侧上台。两只鸡的演员发出"咯咯、咕咕"声，牛发出"哞哞"声，猪在"哼哼"，小狗"汪汪"地叫个不停。)

旁白：老狼"诡计多端"就住在高冈上。他听到了从数千米外传来的声音，偷偷溜进了森林，在树后探头探脑，想弄清到底发生了什么。

(老狼"诡计多端"从舞台右侧上台，慢慢溜到树后。突然间蹿到农场小动物们的面前。)

老狼"诡计多端"：嘿，朋友们，下午好啊！

全体动物：天哪！看我们碰上了谁！（演员们露出害怕的表情。大家向后退一步，跌倒在一起，只有母鸡亨丽塔一人还站在原地。）

母鸡亨丽塔:(她的声音微微颤抖)你好啊,"诡计多端"!

老狼"诡计多端":咦,亨丽塔,你们在我的森林里做什么?

母鸡亨丽塔:天就要塌了!我们想把这个消息告诉农夫琼斯,可是,我们没找到他!

旁白:老狼可聪明了,他马上就看到了让全家一周不挨饿的好机会!

老狼"诡计多端":(狡猾地说)噢,亨丽塔,你说什么来着,天要塌了?天啊,这听上去太可怕了!你们干脆来我家避难吧。在那儿,天塌下来都不怕。

公鸡"宝刀已老":(小声说)亨丽塔,这个主意可不太妙!

母鸡亨丽塔:(紧张地向四周张望)嗯,不过,我真不知道咱们该怎么办了。总之,我们不能待在外边啊。

老狼"诡计多端":(伸出双臂表示欢迎)亨丽塔,别担心!要是天塌了,我的家会是世界上最安全的地方。我的老婆菲奥娜超会管家!她每个月能把上百美金变成美食呢。我们的家里从一楼到顶层都堆满了食物和生活必需品！你和你的朋友们在那儿舒舒服服地住上几年都不是问题，保证你们不会挨饿！

母鸡亨丽塔：真的吗？

小猪"惊恐万分"：（轻揉前额）哇，听上去可帮了我们个大忙哟！我们最怕吃不上饭了，现在什么都不用担心了。

老狼"诡计多端"：我的家又暖和又舒服。每个人都有歇脚的地儿哟！

母鸡亨丽塔：这样的话，我们每个人就都有着落了。（在老狼"诡计多端"的胳膊上轻拍一下）你真是个大好人。对不，"宝刀已老"？

公鸡"宝刀已老"：（点头）对的，对的。

老牛"杞人忧天"：实在是太谢谢你了，"诡计多端"。真走运，我们今天遇到了你！你给我们带路好吗？

小猪"惊恐万分"：我觉得这个决定太棒了。一想到我们安全了，我就开心。而且，马上就到晚饭的时间了。

老狼"诡计多端"：（微微一笑，在前面带路）来，往这边走吧。欢迎你们来到新家！

（小动物们跟在老狼身后在台上转圈，一边走，一边发出很大的声响。)

旁白：就这样，老狼"诡计多端"带着这帮被吓昏了头的小动物们上了路，他们穿过森林，来到了他的狼窝前。就在小动物们正要进去的时候，农夫琼斯刚好从超市回来遇到了他们。

(农夫琼斯从舞台左侧上台。老狼"诡计多端"退后一步，举起了手。)

农夫琼斯：嘿，嘿！站住，都站住！亨丽塔，你们在干什么啊？

母鸡亨丽塔：天要塌了！我们本来想去告诉你这个消息的，可是，没找着你！老狼"诡计多端"建议我们去他那儿躲躲，那里更安全。你要不要和我们一起藏起来？

农夫琼斯：你是怎么知道天要塌下来的？

母鸡亨丽塔：是这样的：我先听到了天空裂开的声音，紧接着，一大块天就砸在了我的头上！

农夫琼斯：那块天砸下来的时候，亨丽塔，你在哪儿呢？

母鸡亨丽塔：我正在苹果树下做着美梦呢。

农夫琼斯：砸在你头上的那一块天长什么样子呢？

母鸡亨丽塔：(回忆的时候，把手放在前额上)嗯，让我看看，我能不能想起来，因为事情发生得太突然了！我觉得，这块天又大又圆，而且还红通通的！

农夫琼斯：有没有可能，砸在你头上的其实是个苹果呢？

母鸡亨丽塔：这个嘛，让我想想。苹果是……

公鸡"宝刀已老"：(一字一句慢慢地说)又大又圆，而且还红通通的！

母鸡亨丽塔：哦，这样的话，估计砸在我头上的是……

全体动物齐声说：一个苹果！

小猪"惊恐万分"：你这只笨鸡！差点把我们喂了狼！

老狼"诡计多端"：(搓搓手)对的，她把你们送进了我的怀抱。要是你们和我进去的话，我老婆就可以做晚饭啦！今晚就先让我们吃顿烤鸡吧！

农夫琼斯：快跑！

(农夫琼斯和小动物们从舞台左侧下台。小动物们边跑边发出"咯咯""咕咕""哞哞""哼哼"和"汪汪"声)

旁白：农夫琼斯、母鸡亨丽塔、公鸡"宝刀已老"、小猪"惊恐万分"、老牛"杞人忧天"和小狗"神经过敏"飞一样地跑下了山，跑向了农场！可怜的老狼"诡计多端"和他的老婆今晚只能吃素汉堡了！

全剧终

show出你的发音
争当英语小明星
▶ 地道口语课
▶ 剧本推荐

微信扫码

故事剧场二

豌豆王国

布景和道具

布景：用硬纸板做成城堡，并画出砖墙；用五颜六色的硬纸板当作城堡里的花园。壁炉从硬纸板取材，壁炉里放三根真木条和一盏橘红色的LED灯当作火。餐厅可以由一张小桌子和三把椅子组成。

道具：绣有"P"字母的毛毡料的旗子是赫勒尔德旗手的道具；另外，整场话剧还需要一个用硬纸板做成的巨大的"P"字。桌上摆有三个装满豆子的碗，配上勺子。

演员表

旁白：讲故事的人。

帕特丽夏王后：有点儿霸道的王后。

彼得王子：王后的儿子。

佩内洛普·萝丝公主：一位美丽的公主。

赫勒尔德：一个有点儿滑稽的旗手。

公主群演：至少七个女孩，她们在台上不用说话。

妆容和服装

旁白：衬衫和裤子配披肩。

帕特丽夏王后：王冠配长裙。

彼得王子：衬衫配优雅的马甲和王冠。

佩内洛普·萝丝公主：长裙配披风。

赫勒尔德：一身制服，头戴一顶滑稽一点儿的帽子，上面插一根羽毛。

公主群演：适合参加派对的裙装，每位公主还要戴王冠。

舞台方位

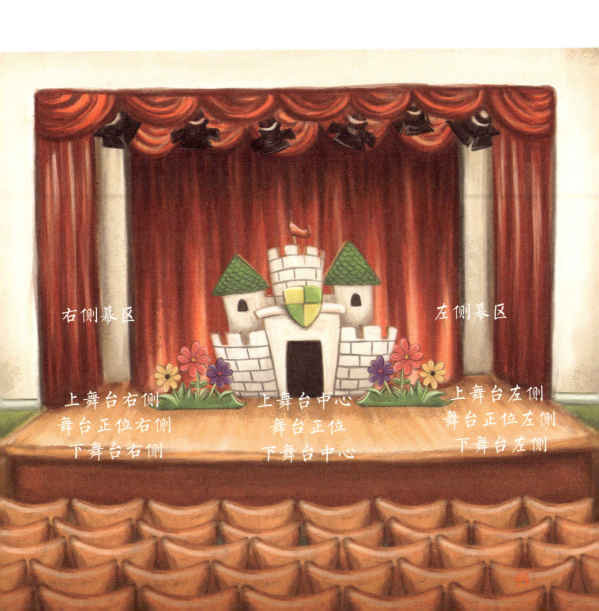

右侧幕区

左侧幕区

上舞台右侧
舞台正位右侧
下舞台右侧

上舞台中心
舞台正位
下舞台中心

上舞台左侧
舞台正位左侧
下舞台左侧

Script: The Princedom of Pea

(Opening of Curtain: A giant letter "P" stands on or above the stage in plain sight. The stage is set with a dining room table, chairs, and fireplace. Queen Patricia and Prince Peter at center stage near table, and Herald at downstage left. Narrator stationed on stool at downstage left through entire production.)

Narrator: Once upon a time, there was a beautiful island. Its fields were green and fertile. It was cool and rainy all year long, a climate that was just perfect for growing peas! In fact, peas were the national vegetable, the main export, and the Princedom of Pea's only claim to fame.

Herald: *(The herald stands at downstage left with his banner and walks across the stage in front of the other actors as he delivers his line and stops at downstage right.)* Peas for breakfast! Peas for lunch! Peas for dinner! Munch! Munch! Munch! Long live the Princedom of Pea!

Narrator: Now, the Princedom of Pea was ruled by Queen Patricia. She had one son named Peter. When

Prince Peter turned 18 years old, his mother thought it was time for him to marry.

Herald: *(The herald stands downstage right and walks across the stage in front of the other actors as he delivers his line and stops at downstage left. He should repeat walking back and forth each time this line is delivered for the rest of the play.)* Peas for breakfast! Peas for lunch! Peas for dinner! Munch! Munch! Munch! Long live the Princedom of Pea!

Queen: We are having a big party. I have sent out invitations to all the eligible princesses in the land. After I have met each of them, I will choose your future wife.

Prince: Oh dear. How many princesses are there?

Queen: Dozens.

Prince: Can't I choose my own wife?

Queen: Don't be silly, darling. Mothers always know best! I will look until I find a princess who is just perfect to rule the Princedom of Pea by your side.

Herald: Peas for breakfast! Peas for lunch! Peas for dinner! Munch! Munch! Munch! Long live the Princedom of Pea!

Narrator: *(Music plays softly. A group of princesses enter from left wing at upstage left.)* And so dozens of princesses came to the palace for the party. But, the

queen didn't think any of them were perfect for Prince Peter.

Queen: *(Pointing)* Too tall, too short, too thin, too meek, too mouthy! And that girl's name doesn't even begin with *P*. Send them all home! *(Princesses exit upstage right into right wing.)*

Prince: I thought some of them were very nice.

Queen: *(Waving her hand)* You are only a boy—what would you know? The future of the Princedom of Pea is at stake!

Herald: Peas for breakfast! Peas for lunch! Peas for dinner! Munch! Munch! Munch! Long live the Princedom of Pea!

Queen: Send for a bowl of peas, please! I need a snack! *(Exit all.)*

Narrator: *(Waving toward stage right at a princess who is knocking on air)* That night, there had been a terrible storm. One of the princesses had trouble on the road. She missed the party. She came to the palace long after all the servants had gone to bed. The prince heard her knocking and opened the door himself.

Princess: I was invited to the palace for the party, but the wheel on my coach broke. Then there was this terrible storm. Please, could you let me come in?

Prince: Of course. You must be freezing. Stand over here by the fire and get warm.

Princess: You are very kind.

Narrator: Even in her wet traveling cloak, the prince thought the princess was very pretty. He hoped that maybe this might be the girl that would please his mother. He introduced himself.

Prince: Hello, I'm Prince Peter.

Princess: *(Bowing)* Oh, I'm so glad to meet you! My name is Princess Rose!

Narrator: The prince's heart sank. His mother had only invited princesses to the party whose names began with *P*. She would never think that a princess named Rose was suitable to rule the Princedom of Pea.

Herald: Peas for breakfast! Peas for lunch! Peas for dinner! Munch! Munch! Munch! Long live the Princedom of Pea!

Prince: I'll call the servants and have a room prepared for you. In the morning, I will introduce you to my mother.

Narrator: And so Princess Rose spent the night at the palace. Prince Peter spent the night dreaming about her sweet smile and her beautiful face. In the morning, they all gathered in the dining room for breakfast.

Prince: Mother, this is Princess Rose. She arrived late last night. Her coach broke down on the road and she missed the party.

Queen: Princess Rose? Princess Rose? I can't imagine why I invited you to the party. Your name doesn't even begin with *P*!

Princess: Actually it does, Your Majesty. My name is Penelope Rose, but my father always calls me Rose.

Queen: Oh, well that is quite a different matter, then. Come and sit beside me, my dear. Let's get to know each other better.

Narrator: And so they sat down to a breakfast of creamed peas. The queen liked Penelope Rose very much and so did the prince. After a lunch of fresh pea salad, Prince Peter took the princess for a walk. They went to see the gardens of snow peas and green peas and sweet peas.

Princess: *(Exit Queen Patricia, herald, prince, and princess walking downstage right away from table)* Don't you grow anything but peas?

Prince: Of course not! After all, this is the Princedom of Pea.

Herald: Peas for breakfast! Peas for lunch! Peas for dinner! Munch! Munch! Munch! Long live the Princedom of Pea!

Princess: So you don't ever eat anything except peas?

Prince: What else would we eat?

Princess: Well, in my kingdom we eat potatoes, beans, corn, lettuce, and squash. There are all kinds of other vegetables and fruits, too!

Prince: There are? I wonder if my mother knows this. I have never eaten anything but peas and I don't think she has either.

Narrator: That night at dinner, the cook served split pea soup. And the prince told his mother about the other kinds of vegetables.

Queen: I've never heard of such a thing! Everyone eats peas!

Princess: I would be glad to have my father send you some samples of some of our other vegetables. I think you would like the fruits as well, Your Majesty.

Queen: But this is the Princedom of Pea, my dear.

Herald: Peas for breakfast! Peas for lunch! Peas for dinner! Munch! Munch! Munch! Long live the Princedom of Pea!

Queen: Nothing will grow here but peas! It's cool and rainy and perfect for peas!

Princess: I think that potatoes and cabbage would grow here, Your Majesty. And also roses.

Prince: What are roses?

Princess: They are beautiful flowers, Your Majesty. They are even more beautiful than the blossoms on your sweet peas.

Queen: What nonsense is this? There is nothing more beautiful than a sweet pea in bloom!

Narrator: The rest of the meal did not go well. The queen sat in stony silence even though Penelope and Peter continued to talk together. That night, after the princess had gone out onto the balcony for a look at the moon, the queen spoke to Prince Peter alone. *(Princess exit upstage right.)*

Queen: It is time to send this girl home. I'm not even certain she is a real princess.

Prince: Well, of course she is a princess! You invited her. She simply arrived too late for the party.

Queen: That is what she told you. You are so young, my darling. Don't be fooled by a pretty face. No one can rule the Princedom of Pea along with you but a true princess.

Herald: Peas for breakfast! Peas for lunch!

Queen: Oh, knock it off and go to bed!

Herald: *(Bowing)* Yes, Your Majesty!

Prince: I like Penelope Rose a lot. I would like to choose her as my wife.

Queen: If there is any choosing, I will do it! I have the perfect way to tell if Penelope Rose is truly a princess. Princesses are very sensitive creatures. Tonight you will hide a pea under her mattress. Only a true princess would feel a pea through a mattress. If she sleeps badly tonight, then we will know she is a princess and you can marry her.

Prince: Oh thank you, Mother!

Queen: She hasn't passed the test yet. I'll bet your Penelope will sleep like a baby and tomorrow morning she'll be packing to go home!

Narrator: Prince Peter was beginning to realize he could never marry Penelope unless he took matters into his own hands.

Prince: *(Grabbing the giant letter P in front of the stage)* My mother asked for a *P* and that's what I will put under Penelope's mattress. Even a peasant would have difficulty sleeping on this!

Narrator: The next morning, everyone gathered in the dining room for creamed peas on toast. Penelope arrived yawning. She had dark circles under her eyes and she looked very tired. The prince began to smile.

Prince: Why, Penelope, what is the matter?

Princess: Oh, Your Majesty, I don't like to complain. But last night my mattress felt so lumpy and bumpy that I couldn't sleep a wink. I am exhausted!

Queen: I don't believe it! Your mattress was lumpy?

Princess: Yes, Your Majesty. It was fine the night before. I can't imagine what happened to it.

Queen: It just shows that you are a true princess, my dear. My son placed a tiny pea under your mattress last night. You are so sensitive that it felt like a rock to you!

Princess: It did feel like a rock—a very large one, indeed. Are you sure it was just a pea?

Prince: *(Nodding and smiling)* Quite certain. I put it there myself!

Queen: I had to make certain you were a real princess before I asked you to join our family here in the Princedom of Pea.

Princess: I'm not sure I understand, Your Majesty.

Prince: Perhaps I can explain. Princess Penelope Rose, will you marry me?

Princess: Why yes, Prince Peter, I will!

Narrator: And so they were married. Gradually Princess Rose brought changes to the Princedom of Pea. She taught her subjects to grow potatoes, beans, and other vegetables and fruits. Prince Peter started a rose garden to remind his subjects of the beautiful princess he had married. And he kept the letter *P* on the mantel to remind him to always think for himself.

The End

show出你的发音
争当英语小明星
▶ 地道口语课
▶ 剧本推荐

微信扫码

剧本：豌豆王国

（大幕拉开：巨大的"P"字母立在舞台上或者放在舞台上方显眼处。舞台上摆放着餐桌、椅子和壁炉。帕特丽夏王后和彼得王子在舞台正位桌子附近，赫勒尔德在下舞台左侧。整个演出中，旁白坐在靠下舞台左侧的板凳上。）

旁白：很久很久以前，有一个美丽的岛国。那里满眼都是绿油油的田野，土壤无比肥沃。那个地方，全年凉爽，雨水充足，特别适合豌豆的生长！所以，豌豆成了这个国家的国菜，而且大量出口海外的豌豆，让这个国家扬名天下。

赫勒尔德：（赫勒尔德举着旗杆在下舞台左侧。边念台词，边带领其他演员穿过舞台，停在下舞台右侧。）早餐吃豆！午餐吃豆！晚餐还吃豆！顿顿香喷喷！顿顿香喷喷！顿顿香喷喷！豌豆王国万岁！

旁白：当下，帕特丽夏王后统治着豌豆王国。她有一个儿子，叫彼得。彼得十八岁那年，王后认为是时候给他选个妻子了。

赫勒尔德：（赫勒尔德举着旗杆在下舞台右侧。边念台词，边带领其他演员穿过舞台，停在下舞台左侧。整场话剧赫勒尔德的台词部分，都需要他重复同样的路线。）早餐吃豆！午餐吃豆！晚餐还吃豆！顿顿香喷喷！顿顿香喷喷！顿顿香喷喷！豌豆国王万岁！

王后：让我们来办个盛大的宴会吧。我邀请了所有适龄的公主来赴宴。我会从她们当中给你选一位妻子。

王子：天哪！要来多少位公主呢？

王后：会来很多的。

王子：我难道不能自己选妻子吗？

王后：哦，我的宝贝，别傻了。当母亲的永远是最有眼光的！我会为你选一位配得上豌豆王国的完美新娘。

赫勒尔德：早餐吃豆！午餐吃豆！晚餐还吃豆！顿顿香喷喷！顿顿香喷喷！顿顿香喷喷！豌豆王国万岁！

旁白：（轻奏背景音乐。一群公主从左侧幕区进入上舞台左侧。）就这样，一大群公主来到王宫赴宴了。

然而，王后觉得没有一个女孩配得上她的小王子彼得。

王后：（手指着公主们说）这个太高了，那个太矮了，太胖了，太听话了，还有那个，嘴太碎了！噢，这个公主的名字竟然不是"P"开头的！让她们都回家去吧！（公主们走到上舞台右侧，从右侧幕区下台。）

王子：我觉得她们里面有几个挺不错的啊！

王后：（挥挥手）你一个男孩知道什么？你的婚姻关系到豌豆王国的未来啊！

赫勒尔德：早餐吃豆！午餐吃豆！晚餐还吃豆！顿顿香喷喷！顿顿香喷喷！顿顿香喷喷！豌豆王国万岁！

王后：来，给我上碗豌豆！我得吃点儿点心啦！（所有演员退场。）

旁白：（朝舞台右侧做出敲门状的公主挥手）那个晚上，起了一场风暴。一位公主被困在了路上，错过了这场盛宴，直到王宫上下的人都睡着了，她才赶到。王子听见了她的敲门声，亲自开了门。

公主：晚上好，我是被邀请来赴宴的，可是，我的马车的轮子坏了，后来，我又遇到了大风暴。你可不可以让我进来呢？

王子：当然可以了。你一定冻坏了吧。来，到壁炉旁取取暖吧。

公主：你真好。

旁白：即使披着湿漉漉的斗篷，王子还是一下子就注意到，这个公主美貌绝伦。他觉得，选这个女孩子做妻子，可能会让他妈妈满意的。于是，他上前一步介绍自己。

王子：你好，我是彼得王子。

公主：（躬身行礼）噢，很高兴认识你！我是萝丝公主！

旁白：一听到她的名字，王子的心就凉了一半。他的妈妈只邀请了名字以"P"开头的公主。她无法想象，一个叫萝丝的女孩怎么能配得上彼得，并和他一起统治这个王国。

赫勒尔德：早餐吃豆！午餐吃豆！晚餐还吃豆！顿顿香喷喷！顿顿香喷喷！顿顿香喷喷！豌豆王国万岁！

王子：我去叫仆人给你准备个房间。明天早上，我会把你介绍给我的妈妈。

旁白：就这样，萝丝公主留在了王宫过夜。彼得王子整晚梦到的都是小公主甜甜的微笑和她的美貌。

第二天早上，大家聚在一起准备吃早饭。

王子：妈妈，这就是萝丝公主。她的马车坏在了半路，所以，她昨晚刚到这儿，错过了宴会。

王后：萝丝公主？萝丝公主？我真不知道为什么会请你来赴宴。你的名字甚至都不是"P"开头的！

公主：尊敬的王后陛下，事实上，我的名字是"P"开头的。我的全名是佩内洛普·萝丝，不过，我爸爸经常叫我萝丝。

王后：这样啊，那就是另一回事了。来，坐在我身边吧，亲爱的公主。让我们来彼此认识一下。

旁白：他们坐在一起喝奶油豌豆汤。王后和彼得王子都非常喜欢萝丝公主。新鲜的豌豆沙拉午餐过后，王子带萝丝公主去散步了。他们去花园里欣赏荷兰豆、青豌豆和甜豌豆。

公主：(帕特丽夏王后下台，赫勒尔德、王子和公主在下舞台右侧远离餐桌的地方表演) 你们除了豌豆就不种别的了吗？

王子：当然不种别的了！要知道，这是豌豆王国啊。

赫勒尔德：早餐吃豆！午餐吃豆！晚餐还吃豆！顿顿香喷喷！顿顿香喷喷！顿顿香喷喷！豌豆王国万岁！

公主：也就是说，除了豌豆，你从来没吃过别的菜？

王子：还有什么可以吃的吗？

公主：当然了。在我的国家里，我们还吃土豆、别的种类的豆子、玉米、生菜和南瓜。总之，有各种各样的水果和蔬菜呢！

王子：真的有吗？我在想，我妈妈是不是知道，世界上还有其他的水果和蔬菜呢。除了豌豆，我从来没吃过别的食物，估计她也没吃过。

旁白：当天晚上，御厨做了豌豆汤。王子一边吃，一边把萝丝公主告诉他关于别的蔬菜的事情，讲给了帕特丽夏王后。

王后：我从来没听过这种事！全天下的人应该是顿顿吃豆的！

公主：如果允许我爸爸给您寄一些我们吃的蔬菜，我会很荣幸的。我觉得，尊敬的王后陛下，要是能寄点儿水果来，您也会喜欢的。

王后：可是，亲爱的公主，这里是豌豆王国呀。

赫勒尔德：早餐吃豆！午餐吃豆！晚餐还吃豆！顿顿香喷喷！顿顿香喷喷！顿顿香喷喷！豌豆王国万岁！

王后：这儿除了豌豆种不了什么别的菜！这么凉爽、雨水充足的地方最适合豌豆生长了！

公主：尊敬的王后陛下，依我看来，这里也适合种土豆和卷心菜。玫瑰在这儿也会长得很好的。

王子：什么是玫瑰？

公主：尊敬的王子殿下，玫瑰是一种很美的花。它比您的豌豆花要美出千倍。

王后：胡说！世界上没有什么花能胜过盛开的豌豆花了！

旁白：后半顿晚餐的气氛很不好。尽管佩内洛普公主和彼得王子继续聊着这个话题，王后却冷冰冰地一言不发。当天晚上，公主出去到阳台赏月时，王后把王子单独叫到了身边谈话。（公主从上舞台右侧下台。）

王后：是时候让这个女孩回家了。我根本不能确定，她真的是个公主。

王子：妈妈，她当然是个公主了！是你邀请的她啊。

她只不过迟到了罢了。

王后：这不过是她的一言之词。你真是太年轻了，我的孩子。别被一张漂亮脸蛋骗得神魂颠倒。只有真正的公主才可以和你一起统治我们的豌豆王国。

赫勒尔德：早餐吃豆！午餐吃豆！

王后：哎呀，好了，好了，下班了，赶快去睡觉吧！

赫勒尔德：（躬身行礼）遵命，尊敬的王后陛下！

王子：我特别喜欢佩内洛普·萝丝公主。我想娶她为妻。

王后：决定你的妻子的人应该是我！我有一个好办法，可以知道这个佩内洛普·萝丝是不是真正的公主。公主是最敏感的了。今晚，你在她的床垫下藏一粒豌豆。只有真正的公主，才能隔着那么厚的床垫感受到那粒豆子。如果今晚她睡不好觉，我们就知道，她是个地地道道的公主了。只有这样，你才可以娶她。

王子：哦，我的妈妈，谢谢您！

王后：别那么早谢我，她还没通过考验呢。我敢肯定，你的佩内洛普会睡得像个婴儿那么沉，明早天一亮，她就得收拾行李走人了！

旁白：彼得王子意识到，如果他不亲自负责这件事情，就永远没机会迎娶佩内洛普公主了。

王子：（抓起巨大的"P"字母抬到舞台前）我妈妈想要个"P"字开头的公主，好，那我就把这个字母放在佩内洛普公主的床垫下。躺在这么大的东西上，连农夫都很难入睡，更别说小公主了！

旁白：第二天早上，大家都聚在了饭厅吃早饭——豌豆酱配面包片。佩内洛普哈欠连天地走了进来。她的眼睛下有层深深的黑眼圈，她看起来疲惫不堪。彼得王子微笑着问候她。

王子：哦，佩内洛普，你没睡好吗？

公主：尊敬的王子殿下，我不是个爱抱怨的人，可是昨天晚上，我的床垫疙疙瘩瘩的，就因为这个，我一夜都没合眼。现在，我累极了！

王后：难以置信！你说，你的床垫疙疙瘩瘩的？

公主：是的，尊敬的王后陛下，前一天晚上还挺好的，可是昨晚糟糕透了。我真不知道怎么会这样。

王后：亲爱的，这说明，你是个地地道道的公主啊。我儿子昨晚在你的床垫下放了一粒小豌豆。你那么敏感，所以，睡在上面就像睡在石头上一样难受呀！

公主：感觉起来就像睡在石头上，而且，是很大的一块。您肯定，只放了一粒豌豆吗？

王子：(点头微笑) 当然肯定了。是我亲手放在那儿的呀！

王后：在允许你成为我们豌豆王国皇室的一员之前，我得确定，你真的是位公主哟。

公主：尊敬的王后陛下，我不太明白。

王子：或许，我可以给你解释清楚吧。佩内洛普·萝丝公主，你愿意嫁给我吗？

公主：愿意，彼得王子，我愿意嫁给你！

旁白：于是，他们举行了盛大的婚礼。在萝丝公主的努力下，豌豆王国慢慢地发生了变化。她教会了臣民种土豆、其他种类的豆子、蔬菜和水果。彼得王子也建了一个玫瑰花园，来让他的臣民记住他美丽的妻子。他还在壁炉上刻上了大大的字母"P"，来提醒自己，要敢于做出决定和改变。

全剧终